# SOFT SPOT, ROTTEN SPOT

### A Collection of Poems

BY
EFE ORAKPO

Pageleaf Publishing Ltd
www.pageleafpublishing.com

Copyright © 2025 by Efe Orakpo

First published in the United Kingdom by Pageleaf Publishing Ltd., London

This is a work of fiction. Names, characters, places, and incidents are either the product of the author's imagination or are used fictitiously. Any resemblance to actual persons, living or dead, events, or locales is purely coincidental.

All rights reserved. No part of this book may be reproduced, distributed, or transmitted in any form or by any means, including photocopying, recording, or other electronic or mechanical methods, without the prior written permission of the publisher, except in the case of brief quotations embodied in critical reviews and certain other noncommercial uses permitted by copyright law.

ISBN (eBook): 978-1-917833-05-9
First Pageleaf Publishing Electronic Edition: October 2025

ISBN (Paperback): 978-1-917833-06-6
First Pageleaf Publishing Print Edition: October 2025

Printed in the United Kingdom

# CONTENTS

07  SATURDAY WOMAN

23  LADY INFATUATED

41  BROKEN SISI

67  THAT GIRL IN BLUE

85  LASS LOST IN A MAZE

# Playlist Note

Each poem has been matched with a song that issues a deeper connection to its verses. Some people may find reading with music a bit distracting, and to others, the option is inaccessible; therefore, the playlist is NOT a necessity and can be ignored.

For those whose preference is to read while music plays, you can listen to the playlist before, after or as you read Soft Spot Rotten Spot. It is entirely supplementary, and as such, it neither takes away from nor adds to the experience.

All 70 songs are available on a Spotify playlist, which you can easily access by searching **"Soft Spot Rotten Spot"** on the Spotify app or web player.

I hope you enjoy listening to it as much as I enjoyed curating it.

Yours rottenly,
Efe

*For the writers who do not write,
the dancers who cannot dance,
and the singers who will not sing;
you are not alone.*

*Dear Dee,
Never put out your fire. Burn steady. Burn bright.*

# I
## SATURDAY WOMAN

*Dream, my sister.*
*You can do it!*
*Dream.*

# Melissa

Juicy limes and lemons
Early morning sermons
Sweet, bland and sour
Intoxicated with power
Noon, night and day
Oh, come what may!
I will love with glee
Love you, my honeybee

# All hail to the Queen

To a perfect perception
And an imperfect reality
To the scent of colours
And the texture of sounds
To the emptiness that looms
And a confidence untold
To the ones I wanted
Who never perceived me
Viva la Reina!

# Chocolate Milkshake

**Ingredients**
2 drops of sweetness
1 teaspoon of empathy
1 teaspoon of patience
1 tablespoon of honey
5 tablespoons of joy
2 serving spoons of faith
2 cups of forgetfulness
5 cups of love
7 cups of loyalty
1 litre of conviction
2 litres of hope
Dash of stature
Handful of humour
Bowl of procrastination
Pound of chocolate
Keg of determination
Barrel of self-will
Sarcasm (season to taste)
Money (spray generously)
Milk (as desired)

**Instructions**
1. Mix the ingredients in order
 In they'll go, one after the other

2. Into a cauldron, be sure to stir well
 Boil for 45 minutes, the scent will tell.

**Notes**
You can't go wrong with this recipe
As long as you avoid error, impurity

Can be served on ice or steaming
A taste will surely leave you beaming.

# Jolly Life

Sometimes I forget to see
All I have inside of me

Hidden strengths, good intentions
A smile that makes connections

Smart ideas, proper talents
An attitude that never relents.

So I remind myself to stop
And take it from the top

Appreciate the little things
Embrace all my blessings.

Take what life offers
And imagine pretty flowers

Because peace within will project
And display itself whole, perfect.

Till there is peace without
And all is calm, no doubt.

Then at that moment
In that very instant

I again begin to see
What I have inside of me

And I truly love it, because
Any other is a counterfeit.

This keeps me fine and dandy
This is my happy remedy.

# Nine Lives

I have stories for days
For the highs and the lows
Sweeter joys and weighty sorrows.
For the laughs shared as love grows
Lessons learned from friends and foes.

I have stories for days
About all the endless drama
And the very occasional karma.
About all the unnecessary trauma
And tales that always have a comma.

I have stories for days
To cheer you up when you're sad
Helping you see that you aren't so mad.
To remember the good times and the bad
While living out the moments you never had.

# Wealth & Riches

She sat thinking and everything else stood still
Her memories chased after one another,
Over and over, until they stopped and gave way
A fond memory, the story of the day she arrived.

In the early hours of a hazy dry day
A few months shy of three hundred
A Saturday in a small town in South West Nigeria
The streets were alive with lights, a city that never sleeps.

She was born in the very centre of all the hustle
The third child to a generous and kind-hearted couple
Healthy and brown-eyed with a head full of hair
A true blessing, their tiny good-luck child.

Their hearts rejoiced as her cries filled the room
They smiled at each other and called her "wonderful"
As the memory faded and consciousness returned
She smiled as well because she knew she truly was.

# What do you see?

It doesn't fit in the rainbow
But add some glitter and it'll glow
It makes a home of outer space
There's no colour it can't replace
In a room that is cool and dark
You can tell it's made its mark

It's whole and stands alone
To me, it owns the throne
Although it seems void and lost
Close your eyes, have a little trust
You'll find tiny streaks of colour
Dancing behind its thin armour

Lots of people think it's evil
Some associate it with the devil
I think it's ambiguous, a speck in my palm
What I wouldn't give to read it like a psalm!
High up in the sky, deep beneath the sea
In my soul, my voice, I see it in me

# Professor

Fearless, emotionless, nefarious
Heartless to some, to others, pompous
So many words, both truth and lies
If you search, you'll find it's all a disguise.

In a world of baseless assumptions
Where free will insists we make decisions
Dying to live, all the while living to die
If you watch, you'll know outcomes solidify.

On a mission to exist differently
To create and establish your destiny
Making plans, dreaming big, they're no crime
If you try, you'll see it's a matter of time.

Knowledge is power; power is time
Time is money; money is all
Four in a cycle that governs land and sea
If you learn, you'll have a universal key.

# GREY AREA

everything. anything. nothing
three alike and three different
everything is anything, yet anything is everything
but both are nothing to one who isn't fluent

# OF THE CRUDE
# FOR THE CRUDE
# BY THE CRUDE

Sand, red as wulfenite, and a hundred fallen trees
Clang, crash, bang, a mighty bloody nuisance they be

"Funny how things look good when you're desperate."

Eight words, like a siren when she said them to me
For my grand escape, "Drill," I say, "as far as my eye sees."

# SHALOM ALEICHEM

"Hush! Be still!"
Oh, be still my racing heart!
Away with worry and anxiety

"Do not yield to fear, for I am always near."
In spirit, in thought, never will depart
No more doubt and uncertainty

# *Rhirirhìrì*

You may crush my spirit
You may bend my mind
You may even strike my form; but,
You can never break my soul

For a fire burns in my soul
Steady and bright, yes, steady and bright
A happy youthful soul I ever will be
Free at last, yes, free indeed

# II
# LADY INFATUATED

*A lover A year*
*My lover this year*
*A lover A year*
*I've loved you all year*

# Coven Society

When the beggars play high and mighty
What do I say to Aphrodite?

When there's not one young aristocrat
What do I say to dear Seshat?

For the starry night sky speaks to me
Says, "Look, princes learn archery."

Undeterred, I say to Cupid and Orion,
"Find me a prince who can fire a gun."

# Bittersweet

Love gives and love takes,
It makes and it breaks;
Love is a poison most are willing to take.

Love cures and love sours,
It empowers and it devours;
Love is a therapy for long lonely hours.

# I Declare,

As the alphabet never changes its a - b - c,
So shall I never change my love for thee.
If it be true the tick-tock should cease in clocks
And revving engines lose their vroom,
I shall love thee still, and up till my doom.

As sure as the tonic sol-fa do - re - mi,
I shall cherish every moment I did spend with thee.
If it be true the drip-drop should cease in taps
And roosters lose their cuckoo-roo-koo,
My heart shall hop to thee still, like a kangaroo.

As trusty as the numbers one, two and three,
I guarantee my loyalty to thee shall be
If it be true the bang-bang should cease in guns
And vicious dogs lose their warning woof,
Our love shall remain, ever, eternal, and bulletproof.

# "Nice Guy"

There goes...
Mr "I know what I want" guy
Mr running out of time guy
Mr "So not like the next guy"

Look, it's...
Mr "I want to give you my all" guy
Mr tall, dark and handsome guy
Mr "I can be the one for you guy"

You know that...
Mr "Don't change for nobody" guy
Mr ideal fictitious character guy
Mr "I'm absolutely not a hard guy"

Yes, he's...
My not-so-perfect Mr nice guy

# Idea

Building castles in the sky
With roads we may never travel
And distances we may never cover
So youthful, in favour of spontaneity.

Full of ambition, a budding romance
Dancing in harmony to your sweet melody
Here I am, not a kobo to my name
Building castles in the sky.

# LIVE LOVE LATE

Heat in my heart, air in my lungs
New and healthy, smile on my face
Complement, happy in my mind
Fling flang flung

The connection, energy for my weakness
The difference, trembling in my bones
The freedom, comfort, blood in my veins
Fling flang flung

Skin hot, head light, happy tears that eve
The peace I feel as the night draws nigh
Conductor o wa o my bus stop no far
Fling flang flung

# Jollof War

I am not a preacher of love, but there is this man, and boy oh boy does he take my breath away. I am smitten by him. His voice, his eyes, his laugh, his smile, his heart; oh, bless his heart.

The purest, most divine, most genuine. His childlike soul... I could write a book about that man, one day I might. I could write a song for the people to echo long after we are gone,

Words, melodies could never capture the essence of my emotions, they consume me. If I could talk about him more, maybe I would burn a little less, but my vocabulary is weak, so burn I must.

# Adderall

I can never have conscious, quiet moments
Because the voices in my head never stop.

Words and sounds that sometimes bounce
In wavy and sharp zigzag motions all about.

Other times, they stay stuck in a weird loop
Like a message that was lost in transmission.

Must be nice to have a little peace and quiet
To think and conceive ideas in a calm station.

I often wish for some hours of order, stability
Time when my thoughts of you can blossom.

# Sweet Dreams

Wipe my tears away
When I'm fast asleep
Keep me close to you
Let me feel your peace

In a shallow grave
Lay my love for you
Dig it up, my dear
Keep me close to you

Steal a treasure chest
Full of gold and jewels
On our stolen throne
Lay my love for you

# ONI
# IGEDE

Man dey go, Man fit come
Dem dey follow any beat wey I drum

Man fit come, You go stay
Na my prayer every day

Man go stay, Me I know
Say na you I wan follow go

Man sef know, Me I dey sing
I no dey hide my love for you, my darling

Man dey sing, Me I hear
But I like your own music pass, my dear

Man sef hear, Me don go
Come back to you and your afro

Man don go, Man dey come
But na only you fit make me beat my drum

# 2010

I had a game; she had one too
I learned hers, each and every play
I gave all I had to acquire a joy so blue
Left with nought but a little wood and clay

Now...

I see her everywhere, no one knows
I hear her name in the faintest tone
I'd like to feel her, burn in her infernos
Scorched in the hope that my heart she will own

## V⁴

Life, you would say, is ordinary. Our cosmos is an extraordinary system with ordinary beings who exist but do not live. How can such ordinary beings comprehend a thing they do not know? How could an ordinary being tell they are void of life if all they know is death?

To live, I would say, is to love. The colours in the sky, the power of wind, the heat of a fire, the texture of earth, and the depth of waters. All extraordinary elements. Crafted to perfection, detailed with attention, alive, loved. How may we ordinary beings ever compare?

Love, the scriptures say, is without fear—an expression of the supreme being. To live in love is to live in divinity. Perfect, unconditional, sure, whole. Finding good love in one's ordinary life makes for the extraordinary. How do ordinary beings take such simplicity and make it complex?

To love, I dare say, is to be alive. Days become brighter, music makes sense, the air feels lighter and smiling comes easy; dancing comes from the heart, rest is good, and all becomes well. A being alive cherishes everything. How can we—ordinary beings—live?

Did you, an ordinary being, deem my love worthy of unequivocal aspiration? Would you, an ordinary being,

choose to live on my account? For I, an ordinary being, have felt a truly extraordinary thing.
Vivo vivere vixi victum! Oh, how you loved me to life!

# Olori
# Ebi

"Nothing good comes from the past," they said, "don't look back at your lover."

"It's in the past for a reason," they said again, "please stay away from that brother."

"I've heard a voice ever so clearly," I said, "though it could be him or the other."

"Won't forget any of the words," I said again, "I'll be careful not to pull that lever."

# Fwd:

I used to think he was perfect—good as new.
I used to say that he was written by a woman, and now I know that was true.

I was the woman. I wrote him. He wasn't real.
He wasn't you.

# III

# BROKEN SISI

*You would say, "S'agapó!" every night.*
*Yet, every break of day, I'd reconcile myself to the fact*
*that I could never say it back.*

# Drink up!

A toast to the ones I touched who crashed and burned, you deserved better

Seven hearty cheers to good love that will be learned, and a happiness greater

# SAFE.

"He disarms me," I thought, "and he puts me at ease."
It was 12:20 on the 1st of February.

...

I smiled a great big smile, lost in thought, humming a song he'd sung to me, "Everything reminds me of him," I sighed. It was 03:32 on the 4th of June.

# Slow Burn

The sky was bright and blue
The day was slow and yellow.
Basking in my youthful flame
I felt the coolness of your timid aura.
Nothing was out of place and
I didn't think I'd have to remember
The day that I met you.

        I'd had my fun and some.
        Spontaneity fuelled my nerves.
        Panic, anxiety, headaches and more
        Tugged at the chords in my lungs.
        The emotions that held me captive
        I'd run into all but one before
        The day that you saw me.

                Night fell quietly, swift as a flash
                I knew something was missing.
                My safe, broken, and to my surprise
                I saw my gem on sale in a vitrine.
                A black Friday like no other, because
                Now I realise, our hearts knew it
                The day that we let go.

# Jinxed

When you called me your lucky charm,
I should have told you I knew it wouldn't last.

I should have warned you about that phrase
About all the others who had thought so too.
I should have warned you about my fortune
About a future where there'd be no me and you.

I should have told you I really wasn't after all,
When you called me your lucky charm.

# Shards

In that moment. Wild and passionate.
Void of thought. Rhythm and ecstasy.
Just one statement. Blunt and crude.
Broke my heart. Through and through.

Silently we sit. Tears and hostility.
You look distraught. Tired and confused.
Never would've thought. Me and you.
Worlds torn apart. Through and through.

# MIDNIGHT

Do you believe in soulmates? I do not
I believe in the wind and the trees
The land and the seas, birds and the bees

Do you believe in soulmates? I do not
I believe in the good and the bad
The happy and the sad, lady and the lad

Do you believe in soulmates? I do not
I believe in the imitation and the gold
The silent and the bold, new and the old

Do you believe in soulmates? I do not
I believe in good love that will last
A connection fast, love from the past

# FANCY ME

Guess what I found? A guy who cares for me
Sweet and soft with eyes as brown as honey

Sees me, hears me, gifts me, serves me, speaks life to me every day
Likes me, loves me, spoils me, draws me, sings to me after a long day

Strong and wise with a warm disarming smile
Often forgets himself but that's okay, he has me on speed dial

I wasn't asking for too much, now I know, but it's time to let him be
It would be naive to think I'd get to keep a guy who fancies me

# "MARK MY WORDS"

Staring at the frame in my hands
Relic of an affair no longer

"What do you long to see?" He asked
I said, "The lights in the North over the sea."

Caught my reflection in the glass
Portrait of a doe-eyed lover

"Where would you like to go?" He asked
With a twirl and a hop, I said, "Where roses grow."

# NEVER WAS
# NEVER WERE

Refusal to wait in line and be redeemed
Became a decision I'm sure you regret.
A shadow, as fate would have it, beamed
New yet regular, much to your surprise.

A star, bright as the noonday sun
Shone and glowed that very yellow day
Together from then on like a bullet and gun
Created a fantasy one might consider short-lived.

Unavoidably, it all ended in this very state
Could have at least tried, held fast, held on
As sometimes it does work out, but I won't debate
You shouldn't either, we were over before we began.

# ONE IN A PAIR

Somewhere in time,
I hope my soul sings with yours to a piano-like rhythm.

In another life,
I hope my being accepts the love you give as you so
long for.

In a different world,
I hope I play the clarinet rings with a heart that loves you.

In an alternate universe,
I hope I hold your hands in love as true as in friendship.

Someday over a cup of tea,
I hope you can admit I was never the right person, it was
always the wrong time.

# HALF-TIME

Emotions raw and feelings that draw
A picture of when I was his January
Days in scores and many moons more
Since I said I loved him back in February

I made a list of things with a crazy twist
Convinced myself they all could March
But the sweetest mist, I couldn't resist
Had them covered, forgotten, by April

Staring at the sun as life takes a turn
While another chapter ends this May
I promise I'm done with all I had to learn
So I'll start anew, all for you, next June

# CRUSHED

Songs that were never sung
Tunes that were never made

Memories and old adventures
Thoughts behind silly smiles

Daydreams with one theme
Stories, charades, and laughs

My feelings will remain untold
For night falls when the day runs

# FRIEND ZONE

The subtle engagements here and there
The grand platform that we both share
Can you see it too?

The body of my words pop-up on your screen
The fragrance of my interest lays in between
Do you see them the way I do?

The repulsive force that plagues our existence
The probability that our book is just a sentence
Take a look from my point of view.

# LIMERENCE

Do I love you too little?
Do I love you too hard?

I think of you at the break of day
When the clouds seem pretty fluffy

I think of you in the dead of night
As the wind sings me to sleep

I think of you when it's hot at noon
And the waves wash over my feet

I think of you in the cool of eve
When the rain drops in trickles

Do you think of me like I do you?
Do you love me like I love you?

If only my heart could write the things it feels for you
If only the mind could fathom the ways of the heart

# STAR CROSSED

We met by chance
After the introductions
After all formalities
Came our mode of dance.

We left, yet ever bound to meet
To have more in common
To have a mutual bond
Our peculiar reason to greet.

The yearning led to further inquiry
Our interactions
Our conversations
This was a bond that wasn't weary.

The wait in vain and in pain
My excuses and care
My anger and hurt
All these caused an emotional drain.

Yet I'll wait
Yet I'll hope
Yet I'll watch to see
Yet I'll listen closely.

Waiting, yearning
Praying, hoping
For what might never be.

# STAND UP

Thinking, considering...
Should I give him another chance?

Hoping, observing...
It had better not be a wasted dance!

Planning, deciding...
I will give him one last chance.

Knowing, perceiving...
It has to be our very last dance.

# EXPERIMENT '98

My heart would flutter
My soul would sing
My eyes would ignite
But not anymore

I've fallen from cliff to sea
Walked blindly into walls
Reached out to folded arms
But not anymore

You're in, you're out, while I hang about
It's been fun you see, and I hope you agree
These games you play were fun yesterday
But not anymore

# CYCLES

"The woman cannot be saved, my lord.
She is yet to learn her lessons. A savage!"
The judge, the jury, cast their gazes on me,
"What do you have to say for yourself?"
"Don't you see? The woman is lost, my lord."
Their inquiring eyes pierced my soul.

I paused. Took a breath. Wore a smile.

"My lord, if I may, the prosecutor and me...
The prosecutor is my lover, my lord, I must say."
Whispers and two bangs of the gavel followed,
"The prosecutor and I have scores to settle,
And in truth, I am not nearly beyond redemption.
This is no trial. It's a witch-hunt, I have to say."

# ROSES & WINES

Only took me a year,
A year and a half to look back,
I always thought I'd done too much,
So I faced my front.

Now that I've paused,
To feel the wind, touch the grass,
Smell the roses, admire the grand sky,
Everything is clear.

It's clear that not only did you do nothing,
I did too much.
I was too sweet.
I was the funny one.

I was the effort.
I was charming.
I was everything, and you?
You were just... Well... You were boring.

# LESSON #1

The plan,
My plan, was to have fun,
To not fall for you, no feelings involved.

The plan,
Our plan, was to just go with it,
To see where the tunnel would end, but
Things didn't go as they were supposed to,
Things didn't go according to plan.

The plan,
Fate's plan, the day we met,
The moment lips sealed our fate.
That day, the beginning of the end.
Little did we know the end was much closer than we thought.

The plan,
My reason, I felt safe yet in danger,
I was on the clouds yet down in Hades,
I was royalty yet a commoner,
I was yours, and yet, never yours.

The plan,
My way—lost, but now, I've found it.
My dream, has changed.

## *Sisi dearest,*

Best believe it was high time you moved on.
No more worry and distress
You're now on merry express
Away with hopeless confusion.

"What do I gain if he knows?"
"Will he soon find out?"
"Does he know what it's all about?"
"Could I ever have him to myself?"

The questions you had, endless
No one had the answers but him
Now...
You couldn't ask him.

You'd lose all confidence and pride.
In his presence, you would shy away
Speaking only when spoken to
Moving only when required to

Your insecurities prevailed above all.
How would you escape from that cell?
And...
You couldn't have him.

A pretty lady took him.
And the things she did, you could not
Never because you were incapable
But because they were unacceptable
Against your morals, a crime by the law, and so

You moved on, accepted your fate
Ignored the truths in your heart
Your mind locked them out but
His name remained with you, forever and always.

His impressions and memories faded
Gradually, you're forgetting about him
Because...
You couldn't love him.

You'd never rest assured of anything
That was the saddest reason of all.
So you let go, began to love yourself
And you've learned by loving yourself
You can finally—properly, love others.

# IV

## THAT GIRL IN BLUE

*I'm not sure;*
*this time,*
*I'm going to make it.*

# HIP HIP HIP HURRAY!

As a young child, oh, how I longed to be 10
And on the first day of that new year
I claimed the new age without hesitation.

When I was 15, oh, how I longed to be 16
Quince to sweet, such a golden time
That year sped by with a great acceleration.

After I turned 16, oh, how I longed to be 17
To be "young & sweet," like that one song
So much so that I look back in admiration.

Loved being 17 and was in no rush to be 18
It took some getting used to, no doubt
Everything was new, fuelled by commotion.

Barely figured 18 out but then I had to be 19
Like a blurry journey to self-discovery
A long dream that held my true ambition.

Bittersweet it is, 19's gone and I get to be 20
Can't say who I'll become or what I'll do
But knowing me... Oh, how I'll long to be 21.

# ROBO WARDEN

Red, yellow, green
Ready, steady, go
With my eyes, I have seen
Now, there's nothing left to show
In my mind, I've been mean
So, I have to let the world know
I'm okay; you'll never come clean
And I've let the hatred grow
Though I gave my heart to sin
It's time to let the wind blow
Red, yellow, green
Ready, steady, go

# IMPOSTOR

I look in the mirror and I don't recognise the person staring back at me.
Who is she?
Why does she look at me that way?

I look in the mirror and I don't see myself in her, she doesn't look like me.
If truly, she is me, then who am I?
Who have I become?

I look in the mirror and I don't see her energy, her shine, her personality.
There's no light in her eyes, is she okay?
Why the long face?

I look in the mirror and I don't think I can accept that she is my reality.
Why would I want to be her?
Why should I stay and be her?

# OCTOBER '20

They see us, but they don't
They hear us, but they don't
A scene we keep reliving
A game we keep repeating
My voice holds a pain it cannot hide
My mind keeps plotting my escape
Do you see us? Can you hear us?

Chaos after crisis, day after day
One bleeding heart after another
Did you see us? Could you hear us?

We scream into the darkness
We speak into the light
We hope for the future
We struggle through today
The weights of yesterday
Should never see tomorrow
Can you see us? Will you hear us?

# ROBBED

As I lay you down to rest
May I have one last embrace
For your heart was my resting place.

Oh, death! You whom I detest
You have taken my lover away
And I do not wish to live another day.

# RUN, MY SPIRIT!
# FOR I'VE LOST MY MIND

Take me away
To a place without sorrow
To a place where there's no tomorrow

Take me away
From the demons of my past
From a happiness that does not last

Take me away
For I have nothing left to give
For this 13th reason, I do grieve

# WALKING DEAD

My strength failed
On our way to the hospital that day
I held her arm, as she led me in
My strength failed

My lungs weakened
In the emergency ward that Sunday night
I managed deep defeated breaths
My lungs weakened

My spirit chilled
On the hospital bed, I did meet death
Bloody bright she smiled at me
My spirit chilled

My heart stopped
In the doctor's office that accursed May
I felt it, I know it, for two seconds or five
My heart stopped

# A LADY FROM LONG AGO

The undoing of happiness must be how fleeting she is
She blooms and grows just as she comes and goes

The undoing of happiness must be how fleeting she is
She laughs then sighs in her sweet hellos and brief good-byes

The undoing of happiness must be how fleeting she is
She feels like a warm embrace but beats you with a mace

The undoing of happiness must be how fleeting she is
She whispers love to your soul but drops you like hot coal

The undoing of happiness must be how fleeting she is
She left when I was young and so I didn't know her for very long

# OJUJU

The moon comes up and everywhere is silent
I can hear the creature chanting my name
Repeating it while stressing the second syllable
Over and over, it keeps getting closer and closer
At last, it stops right by my north-side window
Leaving room for only a twinkle of light
I'm hiding but it's close enough to hear me
I'm still, waiting, slowly counting my breaths.
The creature, frozen like a mannequin, stands tall
As high up as four floors, dinosaur-like even
Its voice: Louder than a siren, deeper than bass.
Its eyes: Darker than midnight, soul-piercing.
I close my eyes tight and pray to wake up
Nothing happens, but I realise it's a lucid dream
So I try to concentrate, control my subconscious
Change the narrative and end the nightmare
I try but fail and eventually, the creature breaks in.
It finds me then we lock eyes and all I see is evil
As my heart starts racing and I brace myself
I finally wake up, panting, glad that it's all over.

# SHADOW

You can never feel my being
But I am here, there and everywhere
I may frighten you in the dead of night
When of my presence, you are made aware
Although dark and quiet, I am harmless
I move as you do, and all with you I share.

You are my one and only companion
To whom I am eternally bound
So I often wish to be echt like you,
For once to not be there when you turn around,
To walk upright under the noonday sun
All these wishes in me are forever profound.

You describe me in your letters and books
You represent me in your drawings and art
Year after year, yet I'm never correctly delineated
Often viewed as an apparition that's quick to depart
I have, with time, come to understand why this is so,
You perceive me to be ersatz, a thing without a heart.

Now, I will tell you what exactly I am,
I am you, even when you choose to go incognito
Attached to you in every possible situation
I am you when you're being a friend or a foe
Here to replicate all your actions in real-time
I am you, but to be me, you'll have to be Jane Doe.

# HYPNOSIS

My memories are a time machine
So the scent of time lingers at the door.

Their perfume announces their presence
And leaves echoes bouncing all around
Like bubbles from a giant wand.
Their words so warm, I can taste them
And their distant hums are electrifying
Like static shock to my fingertips.
Their gift to me is the soul in their eyes
And a soft bed for my beating heart
Like reality would let me stay.

My memories are a time machine
Yet all we are is loot of time's petty crimes.

# BIG LITTLE WIN

Sinking but cannot drown
Trying to swim though held down
Reaching only just below the surface
Without air and certainly out of place.

Walking far or so it seemed
Transparent barriers, lights dimmed
Looking at several other destinations
All blocked, the barriers' divisions.

Screaming in a soundproof room
Able to hear the echoes of doom
That are trapped in, no way out
Bouncing off the walls all about.

Surrounded but always alone inside
Loneliness, a backstage pass denied
It is a specific state of mind
And a way out poses such a great find.

Getting out though almost slipping in
Inner celebration of the big little win
Like a beautiful expensive mosaic tile
So corners and teeth now hold a true smile.

# ALIVE

I own my memories, my mistakes, my past
I've chosen the path to leave my footprints
I'm in charge of my future and what it holds
As long as I can correctly steer my present.

I cherish my past; it's made me who I am
Shaped me, formed me, built my mind
But now it's only wise that I be set free
And I'm confident indeed, I'll never look back.

I will not bury my past like most people do
It'll be cremated, so it can never be dug up
I'll have a quiet, melancholy casting ceremony
On a hillside where the weather's just right.

A nice environment with beautiful scenery
The very best for my most prized possession
I'll be the only one present, for obvious reasons
With a few other items of sentimental value.

I'll scatter its ashes amid the flowers and grass
And let the wind sweep away whatever is left
Speck after speck of memories, hopes, dreams
Till it's all gone, then when all is said and done
There is only one way I will go... Forward.

# BROKEN

A presence that haunts me
Eyes that taunt me
That voice, ever a threat
To refuel that scar's strength.
Makes me relive those moments
Takes hostage of my memories
To remind me of the pain
No, meaningless but life goes on.
"Get over it" "You're not the only one"
"Move on" "It's over and done"
Being choked, dying silently
Yet smiling ever so brilliantly.
Ruth, that dreadful feeling
Truth, in all that I've kept
Perhaps it's all in my head
Scraps of my complex imagination.

# DESPAIR…

I am exhausted, this isn't who I am.
Tired of everything, both needy and regal.
I can't do this anymore.
I can't continue like this.
It's not working out.
I can't sort it out.
Everything is out of my control.
Everything I say is overlooked.
Underestimated and thought dumb.
Misunderstood and acting numb.

## …ASPIRE

Life is a rollercoaster of excuses
People dancing to the tunes of their muses.
Never have I ever been so exhausted
Never has life ever seemed so dysfunctional.
The beginning looks like the end
The end looks dreary and predictable.
This isn't who I want to be.
I used to be the person I now hope to be
So I long to go back to who I used to be.
As time goes on I hope with my heart to see
That I grow into all I've always wanted to be.

# V
# LASS LOST IN A MAZE

*he cannot love you;*
*if he does not love your Father.*

# SWEET
## 16

It wasn't rushed nor was it slow,
it wasn't rough nor was it gentle
It was breathtaking, mesmerising
Before I knew it I had lost control
I didn't care who, I wanted to

# COLONY

A bus
No driver
But somehow
She moves.

Her passengers? Distracted
Her tyres? Loose
Her bodywork? Poor
But somehow, she moves.

Her history? Rich
Her potential? Great
Her destination? Unknown
But somehow, she moves.

Her tank? Full
Her headlights? Bright
A good push
And somehow, she moves.

Her beauty? Marvellous
Her passengers? Exceptional
Her greatest enemy? Herself
Yet somehow, she moves.

# Siesta

I missed it; I can't believe I really did miss it.
How did it happen? What was I thinking?
Time has passed, but I'm still beyond shocked.

It came, but I was nowhere to be found, so it passed me by.
Time being far spent upon my realisation, I cried.
Being unable to explain why is the worst of it all.

"She mustn't be told" "It's a surprise" "Shhh!"
But I found out, waited, anticipated... It never came
I need to let everything out, a scream, a shout.

How do I move on? My heart bleeds.
After so long, its effect is still so strong.
What happened? What did it do to me?

The pain I speak of cannot be compared.
I need help fast; I see the void coming
And I refuse to be a casualty.

# TICKING

You may think that I don't see it,
You may think that I don't feel it.
You may think that I don't know it,
Simply because I don't show it.

Every minute, and I know it.
You anticipate how I'll blow it.
It's the way, every hour of every day,
You break me in pieces.

I'm shattered though parts of me are irreplaceable.
I gave it all I had and you battered me so bad.
It isn't wrong to not be strong, to be fragile.
As the days go by and the hours draw nigh,
I realise I may never, ever be whole again.

+

Breeze in, breeze out
Come clean, come out
Of the closet you've made your abode
Stop walking by on tiptoes.
Tell the truth and be set free
Confirm proudly for all to see
We're a bit too old for this little game
So fear not mockery or shame.
The choice is yours, not mine
To be one, heavenly, divine
That reality is a fraction of our imagination
Just our introspective affiliations.

# TRICKERY

For me to be free, is to sin
For me to gain freedom, to be seen
No matter how I go about it
Or whom I consult concerning it
The result remains unchanged
For me to be with you, is to be uncaged.
A rush of freedom and boundless recklessness
Unaware, amused, a confused madness
That's how I'd seem in the eyes of one and all.

To you, it's a game, another conquest
To me, it's an adventure, one none can contest.
I might think I need you, I probably don't
You might think you'll need me, you probably won't
To think I was in love, what a lie!
To think you cared, you cheating sly!

They say a leopard never loses its spots
That applies to you and all of your guts
Then again, I may be wrong.
You may not be all that I think of you
But to be truly candid with you
After seriously overthinking
Very honestly speaking
I have no idea what's going on.

# THE PREY
# & HER HUNTER

They say age is just a number
It's just a factor of one's mind,
But I never did believe. Good on me!
They were wrong, or so I would come to find.

Approximately two thousand and one days
Since the confession that shook my world
Our korero, a house of double entendres
With every second's tik willed more to unfold.

So I needed to go, I didn't want it to show
But I needed to know, I didn't want it to grow
The beauty in gentle desire... I admired
A need to take it slow, an urge more so.

I'd been blinded by light's darkness
Slowly drowning in a sea of silence
I feared life's cruelty and discomfort
As I'd been pursuing without diligence.

It's my time to take a stand, glow, shine
To soar above those clouds of doubt
To arrive in grand style and make my claim
Show to all who I am, within and without.

# HOW IT ALL BEGAN

Soft spot, rotten spot
And that's what I've got
Soft spot, rotten spot
A little thing we've all got

# GO WELL

*"Everything will be okay in the end.
If it's not okay, it's not the end."*

— *John Lennon*

# Glossary

**Term: viva la reina**
Definition: A Spanish phrase meaning "Long live the queen!"

**Term: shalom aleichem**
Definition: A traditional Hebrew greeting meaning "Peace [be] upon you!"

**Term: rhirirhìrì**
Definition: An Urhobo word meaning "forever."

**Term: Aphrodite**
Definition: In Greek mythology, the goddess of love, beauty, fertility, marriage and passion.

**Term: Seshat**
Definition: In Ancient Egyptian mythology, the goddess of books, writing and knowledge.

**Term: Cupid**
Definition: In Roman mythology, the god of love, attraction and desire.

**Term: Orion**
Definition: In Greek mythology, a handsome giant who was a skilled hunter.

**Term: o wa o**
Definition: A Yoruba phrase meaning "drop me off here" but literally translates to "it is here."

**Term: jollof**
Definition: A West African dish typically made with tomatoes, chillies, onions, spices, and sometimes other vegetables and/or meat. Preparation methods vary across regions.

**Term: oni-igede**
Definition: A traditional Southern Nigerian drum (mother drum).

**Term: vivo vivere vixi victum**
Definition: A Latin phrase meaning "to live" but literally translates to "I live, to live, I lived, having been lived."

**Term: olori ebi**
Definition: A Yoruba title for the leader of a household meaning "head of the family."

**Term: fwd**
Definition: In modern email lingo, the short form of "forward."

**Term: s'agapó**
Definition: A Greek word meaning "I love you."

**Term: sisi**
Definition: A Naijà word used to describe/refer to a (usually attractive) young adult female person.

**Term: quince**
Context: Quinceañera, a fifteenth-birthday celebration in Latin America marking a female person's transition to adulthood.
Definition: The Spanish number fifteen.

**Term: sweet**
Context: Sweet sixteenth-birthday
Definition: A coming-of-age celebration in North America.

**Term: young and sweet**
Context: References a line from the chorus of the hit song 'Dancing Queen' by ABBA, a Swedish pop group that gained popularity in the 1970s.

**Term: 13th reason**
Context: References the Netflix series '13 Reasons Why' released in 2017.
Definition: 21st-century internet culture slang meaning "the final straw."

**Term: Ojuju**
Context: Typically, "ojuju Calabar."
Definition: In Nigerian mythology, a masquerade-like spirit that lurks in the shadows and frightens young children.

**Term: Jane Doe**
Definition: A fictitious name often assigned to an unknown or unidentified female person, typically used in legal proceedings..

**Term: go well**
Definition: A traditional Naijà greeting meaning "farewell/goodbye."

**Sources consulted:**
Definitions referenced from Oxford Languages (© 2024 Oxford University Press) and Collins American Learner's English–Spanish Dictionary (© HarperCollins Publishers).

# Naijà 101

Naijà (Nigerian Pidgin) is an English-based Creole language spoken as a lingua franca across Nigeria. It has a simplified grammatical structure compared to standard English. There are fewer verb tenses and grammatical rules.

Words are derived from English and various languages indigenous to the Nigerian people. It has also evolved to create new words and expressions to describe concepts that cannot easily be explained in standard English or indigenous languages.

Intonation and tonal speech are essential for conveying meaning and emphasis. Although the structure resembles standard English, the vocabulary is adapted to the language, with slang and metaphors playing a key role in Naijà sentences.

Naijà has several dialects, including Warri pidgin, Abuja pidgin, Lagos pidgin, Port-Harcourt pidgin and Wazobia pidgin. Each dialect is specific to a particular region/state/people and is adapted to suit their indigenous language, accent and style of intonation.

**Naijà sentences and translations as used in SSRS:**

Live, Love, Late (pg. 29)
Nigerian Pidgin: "My bus stop no far."
Standard English: "My bus stop is not far."

Oni-igede (pg. 33)
Nigerian Pidgin: "Dem dey follow any beat wey I drum."
Standard English: "They do my bidding."

Nigerian Pidgin: "Na my prayer every day."
Standard English: "I pray about it every day."

Nigerian Pidgin: "I know say na you I wan follow go."
Standard English: "I'm sure you're the one I want to go with."

Nigerian Pidgin: "I no dey hide my love for you."
Standard English: "I don't hide how I feel about you."

Nigerian Pidgin: "I like your own music pass."
Standard English: "I prefer your music."

Nigerian Pidgin: "Na only you fit make me beat my drum."
Standard English: "Only you can tell me what to do."

Nigerian Pidgin: "Man dey sing/come/go."
Standard English: "Men sing/come/go"

Nigerian Pidgin: "Man fit come."
Standard English: "Men may/can come."

Nigerian Pidgin: "Man/You go stay."
Standard English: "Men/You will stay."

Nigerian Pidgin: "Man sef know/hear."
Standard English: "Men know/have heard."

Nigerian Pidgin: "Me I know/hear/dey sing."
Standard English: "I know/have heard/do sing."

Nigerian Pidgin: "Man/Me don go/go come back."
Standard English: "Men/I have gone/have gone back."

# Acknowledgements

I write for those who can neither find the words nor find it within themselves to express their feelings on record, and so, Soft Spot Rotten Spot (SSRS) is an embodiment of many dreams come true because I used to be one of those people.

Thank you to my friend, Derin, for urging me to write down how I felt and unknowingly inspiring me anew. Thank you to my sister, Annabel, for graciously creating a safe space for me to finish my thoughts and sentences.

I am grateful for my family and friends who support me and hold me accountable, and, of course, my dearest readers who have stuck with me through the years.

# Meet The Author

Efe Orakpo is a Nigerian poet whose work explores themes of love, memory and identity.
Inspired by the languages and cultures she observed while growing up in South-West Nigeria, she seeks to honour those peoples and places in her writing.

Efe's poetry is characterised by its conversational and accessible tone. They often employ repetition and ambiguity to convey their messages, allowing readers to connect with their verses on a personal level. She has been writing poetry since her teenage years.

Her debut collection, "Soft Spot Rotten Spot," is a collection of poems that reveal the intricacies, fragility and beauty of the human mind.

Influenced by poets such as Niyi Osundare and John Pepper Clark, Efe's work draws from both traditional and contemporary poetic forms to explore a wide range of themes.

Efe believes in the importance of revision and often spends weeks or even months refining her poems. You can connect with her on social media @efeorakpo

www.ingramcontent.com/pod-product-compliance
Lightning Source LLC
Chambersburg PA
CBHW071217070526
44584CB00019B/3052